After the Attack

by Barbara Fifer

PEARSON

Scott
Foresman

Editorial Offices: Glenview, Illinois • Parsippany, New Jersey • New York, New York

Sales Offices: Needham, Massachusetts • Duluth, Georgia • Glenview, Illinois
Coppell, Texas • Sacramento, California • Mesa, Arizona

Thousands of people were working in the World Trade Center in New York on the morning of September 11, 2001.

Terrorist Attacks

September 11, 2001, began as a clear autumn morning in the northeastern United States. People were still arriving at work when an airplane crashed into one of the World Trade Center's Twin Towers in New York City. Many people at first thought it was a horrible accident, but eighteen minutes later another plane crashed into the second tower. Thirty-seven minutes after that, a third airliner crashed into the Pentagon in Arlington, Virginia, near Washington, D.C.

Terrorists had overpowered the crews of four airplanes that morning. The terrorists flew three planes into the buildings on purpose because they were angry at the United States and its influence on the world. Passengers on the fourth plane, Flight 93, fought the terrorists and their plane crashed in a field in Pennsylvania instead of into a crowded building.

These were the first foreign attacks on the United States since the War of 1812, when Britain had invaded the United States. Many people became heroes that day. In this book each person's story represents many others who did similar things.

"Twin Towers" and More

Seven buildings around an open space called a plaza made up the World Trade Center. Those buildings stood in New York City near the southern end of Manhattan Island.

Businesses rented space in six of the buildings for their offices, with some large companies occupying more than one floor. About 50,000 people worked in the offices. The seventh building was a hotel.

When the attacks occurred, at least forty thousand people were working in the buildings. During a typical workday, about 50,000 people worked there and about 200,000 visitors might pass through the World Trade Center.

The two most famous buildings were known by several names: the Twin Towers, North Tower and South Tower, or WTC1 and WTC2. Both were 110 stories, or 1,368 feet high, and ranked among the world's six tallest buildings. Each tower had ninety-seven elevators for people and six elevators for freight. The North Tower was completed in 1970, followed by its twin two years later.

Here is a view of the World Trade Center buildings before the attack.

This is a view of the Pentagon, which is so large that the United States Capitol could fit into one of its five sides.

A Building Named for Its Shape

Pentagon is the name given to a five-sided figure. The United States Department of Defense has its home in a building of that shape, which is simply called "the Pentagon." It opened in 1943 and is just across the Potomac River from Washington, D.C.

The Pentagon is five stories tall and covers twenty-nine acres. The total length of its halls is seventeen-and-a-half miles.

The Pentagon is the **headquarters**, or main office, of all branches of the United States military. Working in it are about twenty-three thousand soldiers and civilians, along with about three thousand support staff.

Four Airliners

Around eight o'clock on the morning of September 11, 2001, four airplanes took off with terrorists on board who were pretending to be regular passengers.

The terrorists **hijacked**, or took over by force, Flight 11 from Boston, Massachusetts, and crashed it into the World Trade Center's North Tower about an hour later. Shortly after, the same thing happened to Flight 175, also from Boston, which crashed into the South Tower.

A third plane, Flight 77, left Washington, D.C., and flew as far as Kentucky before terrorists hijacked it. The terrorists turned it back toward Washington, D.C., and crashed the plane into one side of the Pentagon.

A fourth plane, Flight 93, flew from Newark, New Jersey, to the skies above Ohio. A few people on board heard about the first three crashes on their cell phones. When terrorists captured their plane, some passengers decided to fight back. A flight attendant filled two pitchers with boiling water and several passengers tried to break into the cockpit. The terrorists managed to crash the plane in a field in northeastern Pennsylvania. Many people think their real target was the White House or the United States Capitol.

Terrorists crashed an airplane into each of the World Trade Center's Twin Towers on September 11, 2001.

Even though they were worried about their own safety, many Twin Towers workers helped others descend the stairs and get outside.

Office Workers Help Each Other

After the attacks on the World Trade Center occurred, cement dust and burning jet fuel filled the buildings with thick, black smoke. Many people helped one another to escape the buildings.

Michael Benfante and John Cerqueira worked on the eighty-first floor of the North Tower. They felt the building sway from the crash and saw fire outside the windows. They began descending the stairs, knowing that it was not safe to use the elevators.

On the sixty-eighth floor, they met a woman in a wheelchair. Using a special rescue chair they found, the two men carried her the rest of the way down the stairs. It took an hour for them to reach safety.

In the South Tower, Welles Crowther used his training as a volunteer firefighter. He carried some people down the stairs and got dazed people to help others who had been injured by the plane crash. Crowther was working alongside New York City firefighters when the building collapsed.

Other survivors in both towers rescued people trapped under furniture or walls. When people fainted on the stairs, others carried them. Some people formed human chains to help one another over cement slabs that blocked the way.

Firefighters, Police, and EMTs

As office workers made their way down the stairs in the Twin Towers, firefighters and emergency medical technicians (EMTs) rushed up the stairs. Each New York Fire Department member carried sixty pounds of tools along with an oxygen tank.

Outside, other firefighters gathered. They could not reach the fires high in the towers, but they fought smaller fires on the ground. EMTs treated injured people as soon as they stumbled outdoors.

The two airplanes each carried about twenty-four thousand gallons of jet fuel. The fires created by the crashes burned as hot as 460 degrees and weakened the towers' steel frames. Soon, the frames could no longer hold up the heavy concrete. The towers had remained standing after the crashes—the North Tower for about one hundred minutes, and the South Tower for nearly sixty minutes. Thousands of people escaped during that time.

Finally, the towers' steel frames gave way and the buildings "pancaked" down, one floor landing on top of another. Inside the towers, 343 firefighters and 23 police officers were killed. Later that day, WTC (Building) 7 and the hotel also collapsed.

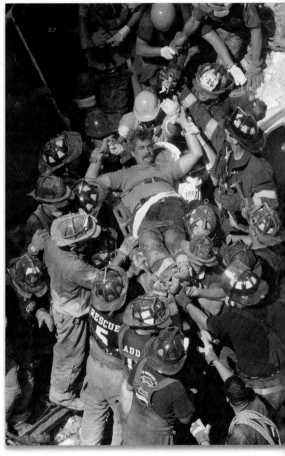

The New York Fire Department crews arrived at the Twin Towers and began rescuing people within minutes.

7

Pentagon Rescuers

The Pentagon has its own police and fire departments, but many other fire departments from Virginia and the District of Columbia also came to help.

Many soldiers who worked in the Pentagon quickly created teams to dig tunnels under furniture and fallen walls, letting people crawl out. One large man from the Navy held up a ceiling while people escaped. No one found out his name.

Army Lieutenant Colonel Victor Correa walked through smoke in a darkened hallway, shouting. Over and over, he yelled, "Listen to me! Follow my voice!" It worked, and he led people outdoors. People remembered him as "the man with the big voice."

Staff Sergeant Christopher Braman, a cook in the Marine Corps, used his search-and-rescue training when he heard a woman clapping loudly. She could not breathe well enough to call for help, and was badly burned. Braman found her and carried her outside, then went back inside to find others.

Fire departments from around the area came to help the Pentagon's own firefighters.

Air traffic controllers watch images of airplanes on computers while they talk with the pilots by radio.

Land the Airplanes!

The Federal Aviation Administration (FAA) sets the rules for airliners and other non-military airplanes. After the first two crashes took place on September 11, the FAA stopped planes from taking off. The FAA also told air traffic controllers to land all planes at the nearest airports.

Air traffic controllers are the people who talk to pilots by radio, guiding them while they take off and land at airports. Air traffic controllers have to be calm in emergencies, such as storms, when pilots need extra help. Now they had to land nearly four thousand planes at once—all over the United States!

Only military planes were allowed to fly, including Air Force One, the President's plane. President George W. Bush had been visiting a school in Florida when the attacks occurred.

No one knew if terrorists had already hijacked more airplanes. If a plane refused to land, it would be checked further.

By about noon, all airliners had landed safely. Only military planes were allowed to fly for the next two days. Airports made stranded passengers as comfortable as they could.

When the Twin Towers fell, they sent a thick, dark cloud of smoke and dust through parts of New York City.

Local Businesses Help

When the Twin Towers collapsed in New York City, they filled the air for many blocks with choking smoke and dust. At that time, thousands of people were walking and running to safety.

Restaurants, stores, and hotels opened their doors. Managers let people come inside, have a drink of water, and use the restrooms. Those services are usually just for customers, but September 11 was different.

Subways and trains stopped running because no one knew if they were safe. People had to walk for miles to get home. Some stores passed out free running shoes to people who had lost theirs rushing down the stairways or along sidewalks.

A fancy hotel set up beds and cots in its ballroom. Hotel workers volunteered to stay and help. The chef started cooking huge batches of food instead of his usual fine dinners. Rescue workers were welcome to eat and rest at the hotel.

When darkness fell, some people were still stuck on the streets. Hotels lent them pillows, sheets, and blankets to use during the cool autumn night.

Searching for Survivors

While people were still escaping on buses and ferries to other parts of New York, rescue workers began digging for survivors at the Twin Towers.

In New York City and at the Pentagon, off-duty police and firefighters arrived from everywhere, along with doctors, nurses, and EMTs. Construction workers brought heavy machines to move the rubble. The first rescue workers to arrive were local, but more and more rescuers came from all around the nation.

Trained search-and-rescue dogs came with their owners—about 350 teams in all. The dogs crawled into small spaces, walked on broken glass, sniffed for survivors, and heard sounds that humans could not.

Spotlights were set up, and rescuers worked around the clock. They found a few survivors. Whenever a person was found alive, rescuers called for silence. All noise stopped until they could locate the trapped person.

Rescue workers searched for trapped survivors at the Twin Towers all through the night of September 11, 2001.

People Donate

Within four days, more than 250,000 people donated blood for Twin Towers' and Pentagon survivors. Usually, in four days, only about 91,000 people donate blood. People who are badly burned or lose blood in accidents need new blood to replace their lost blood and to help them heal.

In New York City, Robin Merendino, her sisters, their mother, and a friend, went to forty restaurants and supermarkets to ask for free hot food for the rescue crews. Soon they had 1,500 pounds of meals! They needed five vans to deliver the food.

The Nation Gives

Companies around the United States began sending the products they make. Toys, clothing, blankets, snacks, and other items began arriving in New York City and Arlington, Virginia. They were for survivors, families of those who died, and rescue workers.

Thousands of people donated blood to help those injured in the attacks.

Individual citizens, companies, and other groups donated many items to survivors and rescuers.

The New York Fire Department lost ninety-one fire trucks, rescue trucks, and cars when the Twin Towers collapsed and crushed them. Residents of cities in Louisiana, Ohio, and Utah bought new fire trucks for the department. Schoolchildren in Columbia, South Carolina, held a fundraising drive that raised money to buy New York City a new fire truck. At least two other trucks were gifts from companies that build fire trucks.

Schools, clubs, and businesses across the United States held events to raise money. They sent checks to bank accounts that had been created for those harmed by the attacks. Some accounts were reserved for educating children who lost relatives, others helped people who had to move out of damaged apartments, and still others were for survivors who needed long-term medical care.

Worldwide Sympathy and Changes

Other nations around the world expressed their sympathy for the United States' losses. "Today we are all Americans," said Benjamin Netanyahu (bean-yuh-MEAN neh-tuh-NYAH-hoo), a former prime minister of Israel. He meant that all nations shared in the sadness of the United States.

Working day and night, people cleaned up the World Trade Center site and trucked away the broken steel and cement. They completed the difficult job on May 30, 2002—three months earlier than expected.

Airports made many changes in how they checked passengers getting onto airliners. They wanted to make it impossible for terrorists to take over airplanes ever again.

Rebuilding and a Memorial

More than 3,000 people died in the four attacks on September 11, 2001. They included airplane crews and passengers, office workers in the three buildings, firefighters, EMTs, and police. More than 2,500 people survived with injuries, while others were not hurt. Altogether, these people were from many states and the District of Columbia in the United States, along with many others from countries around the world.

The last piece of steel was removed from the World Trade Center wreckage eight months after the attacks.

A single tower to replace the Twin Towers will be 1,776 feet tall, commemorating the year the United States gained its independence.

A contest was held to select a design for new buildings to replace the ones that had been destroyed. The new buildings will be built where the Twin Towers once stood in New York, and a memorial will stand beside them. A **memorial** is a way to remember and honor a person or a certain event. The damaged part of the Pentagon was repaired and reopened in eleven months. The National Park Service plans to build a memorial where Flight 93 crashed. Everyone who helped during and after the attacks is a hero of 9/11.

Glossary

headquarters the center of operations for a company or a military unit

hijack to take control of a moving vehicle by use of force

memorial a building, statue, park, or other creation that honors certain people or events

pentagon a shape with five equal sides

terrorist a person who uses violence and fear to try to achieve goals